Pen Leakage

SpitVerb Entertainment LLC

J.L.Davenport

Copyright © 2008, 2013 by Jamelle Davenport
All rights reserved. This book, or parts thereof,
May not be reproduced in any form whatsoever
unless permission is received from author and/or
representative.
ISBN: 978-0-6152-3842-5

J.L.Davenport

CONTENTS

Pen Leakage

    I. Willpower

1. Fallen Angel

2. Black like American, I am

3. Clean

4. Tableau

5. He Gave Roses

6. Resilience Of A Woman

7. Miscegenation, Black Woman, White Man- You Have Words?

8. Men Say Many

9. Monday Morning

10. Thy Sympathetic Wing

    II. Humanity

11. Mechanics of Music

12. Cherish

13. Why?

14. Mirror Mother

15. The Pale Touch

16. Pain

17. Out Of Tune

18. Ignominy

19. Images of Unnecessary Violence

20. Shameful Human

21. Silk Roads of Rivers

22. Don't Cry Tears Unless They Are Smiling

23. Spit Spat

24. Bad taste

25. Feel Right

26. Pushing Me Away

27. Eye Blink

    III. Inequitable

28. Imagine

29. No Will to Forgive

30. Denazify

31. Broken Limbs to Set me Free

32. No Victim

33. Depart The Past

34. Mold Me

Leakage

CHAPTER 1
Willpower

J.L.Davenport

Fallen Angel

If my heart were like my bladder- overfilled
No exit would be sufficient
The aching is the same
Therefore, I cry myself to sleep
Someone whispers out my name and with that it is saying
Your quest is to subsist and be wise
For the body is but a tide on a big wave
Like the first, you must tumble through the skies and open your eyes
Like them, you will have to go
Have loins to conceive your ego
Trials to break your pride
Test to strain your spirit
Your only existence is eternity to mend what has been broken
Paradise
Pain will bring you closer to me
When you cry you call my name
We will be together all the same
How quickly can you find your path?

Leakage

Black like American, I am

I say my mind went empty when I lied and I did lie
I lied for hands to touch me
I lied for arms to hold me
I lied for lips to kiss me
Doesn't mean I'm not comfy in my skin
Just a bit lonely and sad within
I did tell you what you wanted to hear
I'm confident to the other ear it did not reach the wax
Nevertheless, it is the fact that your eyes looked at me
To make my stomach turn a thousand times
Knowing that you wanted me
I was wrong
So I am here to be truthful
Is it permissible that my genetics be of gentility?
I do not know my genealogy
The present doesn't hold the past
My family tree is incomplete
However, do not judge me because
All the family I know and need is with me
My family comes from the cotton fields but my

J.L.Davenport

fingertips are soft and my eyes have never seen cotton grow
I heard it is painful and leaves the body weary
It only broke my family
Left us,
Scattered state to state
My grandma says,
She only wears the cotton
She has not seen it grow and she ain't never plucked them suckers neither
But my grandma's mama use to say,
"There is no job worse than picking cotton
You'd start at night when the sun ain't bright and stop at night in the moonlight
Nothing was good about that cotton, only the cotton pockets it was filling
The body be so weary, your spirit done ran away
It was songs that got them through the daily tortures of the cotton, the boss and the evil."
My grandma says her mama didn't pick any cotton either but her mama's mama did
However, since the cotton came as far north as it was south and the money made, fed as many northern mouths

Leakage

It was no surprise at all the suffering was the same
That little war to set Black people free from slavery was really just about all that money
Lost by the South
Gained by the North
Dying for the dollar as they always did and using Black people as the excuse
Who's making and who's taking
I agree with my grandma and her mama
They like to place that on us black folks too
As if we owe them our gratitude for being set free from centuries of servitude
We are as human as the next man
Therefore, the only thing I know is as far as my family tree can relate,
We as black as night and so pretty in the day
Moreover, to renew my peace inside I recant that petty lie,
Black like American, I am

J.L.Davenport

Clean

If ever I was clean
It was before I was born
Comforted by my mother's womb
Who would have thought to breech this world,
would only be, to be scorned

Tableau

Sleep is a marionette with coffee stained crooked teeth
Keep your eyes open so not to see it
It will smile tragic
Bouncing around, in your head, on strings

Predator; beautiful face, sweet smile, naïve eyes, gullible ears
Could it be so easy?
She could make a man smitten and drive a boy wild
She was unaware
Rape her
Cover her mouth, grab her neck, and pull her hair
Screams are loud when they cannot be heard
It travels through the face
It is seen in the eyes
It is felt in the muscles contracting
Rape her
She moves like an insect so you strike her
Spread her legs so far even you cringe… but you need to enter
There is no time for empathy

J.L. Davenport

There is no time to edify your salacious reasoning
Your loins cannot behave… something warm and fleshy is…
Grown woman thinking aloud: *Rape her in a soiled place and toss her aside*
Open up your mouth you bastard! While she cries
Your shriveling erection dripping in her innocence
Go ahead you bastard and lie to her
Tell her she did not feel like a virgin
Ah, if it were not for all her trouble, it sure would have been some good pussy
As a little girl; *Monster is all she can think ruined is all she feels*
Grown woman thinking aloud: *Years have passed and she still can't sleep and she still feels shattered*
Memories obfuscate her world
A man's smile brings forth her guard
Soft-spoken words from a man are contumely; she would rather hear him obscene
She does not have to speculate his gallop
Death came for you demon and the soil that cakes your bones shudder in disgust
Now you are only dust

Leakage

However, your victim is alive, she is grown and
she is dehumanized still
You left her flesh to burn
Empyreal beauty once
A tattered hymen did not mean so much…
You left her flesh to burn
It will never be precious to anyone
Inflamed, swollen, fleshy and itchy

J.L.Davenport

He Gave Roses

Her body is like a garden unattended
To look upon it and see some beauty and then
shake your head at the intrusion
There are footprints in her soil
That have kicked and pinned her down
Someone has removed her thorns
The only means to protect her crown
Someone underbred has made her bed
Rude and cruel to discard her very essence with
cruelty and in the aftermath leave her with this
story
Rose bushes red and sensational stain her skin
The scrubbing of her bushel to remove his odor
Of funky breath saliva soaking
Hands on her body heavy
Pulling, spreading and scratching
Lilacs slowly bloom
Palms push into the sides of her cheeks
No! She screams
Face contorting ugly just to breathe
Just to breathe and not to see those shimmering
colors
Of polka dots

And sounds of pen needles
The throbbing in her crotch
Elbows in her chest and the smashing of her breast
Body aching screaming where the mouth has no voice
The nascent of a lady still a girl can allure
To obscure her future before she is a woman but still not a lady is repeatedly a curse most girls will nurse
He gave her roses red and sensational
But left her with lilacs to slowly bloom

J.L.Davenport

Resilience of a Woman

Exploitation of the female looks good on the big screen
Big breast, tiny waist, sleek thighs
Debauchery
It don't hurt nobody when the film is edited
Perspiring flesh
Liquid moans, uncomfortable positions
Soaking sheets with spit, body fluids and teeth biting eye bulging
And gorged
Orifices open in pulsating widths
Make that money bitch
Alleviate her weakness, the need for cash
Detour to her intestinal track
Some just like to be fucked rough but most do not enjoy it so much
Hey little man waxing your flip flapper, hard
When you are through doing you, watching the porno *Young Girls and Old Men*
Think about your daughter
And her perky breast, her small stomach and soft flesh
Tossing her hair

Her mind is innocent her demeanor bouncy and giggly
As she should be
A man with no care will steal her virtue and break her heart
A man like you
When you watch, *Hairy Cougars like Big Cock*
Think of your aging mother with her sagging tits
Double belly, because in her womb you were carried
Her cellulite thighs used to be so tight and her ass your father held through the night
However, in all those years the only enjoyment fulfilled is her fingers caress
When you watch *MILFS like 'em Young*
Think of your grandma with her walking stick
Breast paper thin and so is her skin
All the years of hard work and no play
Probably had 10 kids and most of them boys
Moreover, her best days were in admiration of her children
If she only knew what you did
And she does
A mother knows her child

J.L.Davenport

A world built on a mates caress

Then a mother's love

All that love and still a woman is only flesh

Leakage

Miscegenation, Black Woman, White Man- you have words?

Thanks to the heavens, you are not my man
Your bickering is unbearable
The constant complaints on the man I am sleeping with
"You are still sleeping with the Massa!" That's what you say
Well Mr. Slave Minded Imbecile, I have never been owned
You sleep with white women and all across the globe you've had your dick moistened
From Executive to ho stroll
Nonetheless, you have words for me
When back in the day when the ancestors were slaves you would have lost your balls
Even today in some prescient place where bigots have not changed
Yet, you have words for me
"You are still sleeping with the Massa!"
Bla Blat Blab
No Mr. Slave Minded Imbecile I am sleeping with a man who just happens to be white
Let us say I add some color to his world and all

J.L.Davenport

that good stuff
You do it. Why not me?
You do not deserve me with your big lips talking so much
Maybe mañana you'd see I'm still that queen
Let me spit some obeisance your way
Pale, pink or over tanned never lays a hand
His voice is not deep somewhat soft and sweet
Definitely loving and submissive toward me
If he is small with big o' balls he knows how to use it all
His mouth does not speak any bad
Some weird wit but he knows when to quit
When his mouth gets naughty, it is only for the kitty
Dribble, wiggle, tickle and spark a tingle for that kitty
If I am not happy neither is he
Isn't that the way it is supposed to be
What a man
My man
Have you heard a black woman bark?
On the other hand, rearrange opera? Speak in tongues and not to Jesus when in orgasm?

Leakage

Exactly, you would not know
Because your style is to beat the pussy up and probably the woman as well
No doubt
However, my man loves the pussy up, down and all around
Stimulating my brain and then my body
Don't complain about the white man
Because you're big lips just talking and my ears don't want to hear
Some white woman has filled your head with fiction
Hustle and flow is what you know
Get to walking
I say she can keep you and I would not want to be her
Pale, pink or over tanned
The color does not make the man
Did you say pussy's pussy?
Well here is what I say
Dick is dick just a dangling thing

J.L.Davenport

Men Say Many

Many men say many things
Many things many men say
If the dictionary were, the way to warm flesh a man would learn it
Hard work and a paycheck would be perfunctory, less he does not receive that awaiting pussy
Let alone eat
However, a man does not even have to bleed like we, to have warm flesh wet
He will just open his lying mouth and waggle his dick
Show off his practiced walk and experienced talk
Show his last cash and rental vehicle to get you set in motion
What man can see me without a disposition?
Without a disposition, would a man see me?
Genuinely be interested in me?
Can I stay the night?
Can I drive your car?
Can I have the keys to your door?
Let me see
What man can please me before himself, use his

damn mind, and quit manipulating mines
If a man could speak with his eyes
If a man could hear with his heart
If a man could see with his arms
I might stop to listen to all those things they keep saying
Conversely, frank as I must be- just as they are in the sheets
I have had enough
Fixating on intimate memories that left secretions between my legs
On my bed but my craving never fed
Mine eyes never dry because I don't know why he is with me
If he likes me or doesn't like me
Does he want more of me?
Taking, stroking, sucking, fucking heart broken
Waiting, wanting, hoping heart broken
Many men can say many fucking unconscionable, terrific, and tantalizing, body tingling things
With no shame and my emotions cannot endure
Therefore, I am sure I will become a lesbian

J.L.Davenport

Monday Morning

The weak doorbell of early morning birds
Crickets commingling
Last night's rain still dripping
Trees rustling with the yawn of morning wind
Unpleasant sounds of nature awakening you
Along with your alarm clock you immediately smack
It's Monday
Arise
To the sun not yet risen
Or too bright in your eyes
The shower can only deliver you a little
What should I do with my hair?
Dammit! What do I wear?
Coffee or tea…
Dry toast?
Bagel…
Pop tart?
Cereal…
It's Monday
Breakfast never comes easy
Drive -thru
Yes, can I have an egg and cheese croissant, two

hash browns and orange juice please, oh, and some syrup
Slow traffic on the highway
In addition, middle finger man is middle finger happy
Retaliating foot drops on the brakes
Fool… I should have just hit you
In his rearview mirror, he has a devilish smile
Are his teeth green?
A long day waits
What doesn't help is the dreadful job with its spying bosses and gossiping coworkers
The lying, lazy ones too all full of themselves or snacking on their asses

Thy Sympathetic Wing

In and out
Out and in, trite that is what my life has been
most about
That hunger for serenity, confidence, and success
That duty to believe in myself, in life
Stability clinging although in constant change
Eau de my insides are deprived of fulfillment
Then thy sympathetic wing came and swooped me up
Thy wing came and swooped me
My lost legs now dangling to a new propensity
Thy wing glided my pride with a watchful eye and
then laid me down
Wing of prosperity wiped away my frown
Advance and learn, it pushed me on
It pushed me to learn and advance
Options to succeed enormous
Take a feather, whatever supports my needs
Most will never receive this chance
A small chance to be…all that I can be

CHAPTER 2
Humanity

J.L.Davenport

Mechanics of Music

Musicians run blind by the music

Mind and ears dancing with their fingers

Composition swimmingly

The thick wail of the trombones

The thin whine of the trumpets

Tantalizing violins swift and swank

Seducing the saxophone

Approaching, the drums with their gusty ingress to quiet the ablaze

The tranquility rapt in various sanctuaries for those who find serenity in the lustrous sound

Syncopating at a tangent

Musical brilliance reaching climax

Cherish

An isolated glade is the idyll

Where there be fresh air within the brush of trees

Lakes of peaceful waters

Undisturbed

Deep within the solitude

Songs sung by birds

Whistling bees and rainbows of butterflies

Safe and beautiful from destructive hands

Not so many can touch it or get to it

Why?

Drip… Drip

Blood lining the inside of my thighs

Tinkling down with the shower water

A blood clot formed and stretched falls and sits

bleeding wet

Why must I bleed?

Large dark areolas rippling towards

Nipples harden at the slightest touch reaching for

Salvation of a somewhat sensation

Why must I carry these bags?

It once was flat and easy to tickle

To stroke the middle now corpulent all the way

around to the back

J.L.Davenport

Natural to carry a healthy fetus and make a father smile
The world will call it fat
Why must this womb be my nightmare?
Full of heat this folded odd flesh
Wet with odor even when it's clean
Always wanted, a lot of times mistreated, sometimes tasted and seldom satisfied
It is happy only a short time and it affects my every being
Why must my sex make me?

Leakage

Mirror Mother

You didn't save me!
Alone with your liquors breath and large backside
Too religious in the past
Alas got you nowhere but alone just like she
Obese whores and smoky rooms that was she
You left me to a young woman's broken spirit older
in age but still young and broken
Crowded with pain that was she
No heart should feel such clutter but she born you
with that sadness and you born me with it too
Stains of early pain from her surely left a mark on
you
Nevertheless, you left me to inherit that spirit as such
Smiling don't know this face
When it shows it glows but this face does not know
Too much strength and always cold
Too much independence and always bold
No confidence because no one told me so that I
should know to have confidence so
If hell should freeze before it burns that is what I
perceive
Then I will not know
My days are cold in the summer and I have the
winter visits
Now of age and alone

J.L.Davenport

Obsolete has caught up
Even with beauty and angelic spirit
Intelligence and talent does supersede
No comfort of a companion to frame my destiny
My earlier complaints have conformed and I now see
Me

The Pale Touch

To be touched by forbidden hands
Held by pale arms
Kissed by pink lips
Demonic eyes stare thru blue
So close, so many times
Slick incentive
Infinitesimal shivers flow beneath the skin
However, I have yet to reach my peak
Dictatorial motions are stifling
Sweet smile, falsetto tongue
Promises lure my essence with sweet titillation
Gullible my body to have felt all of heaven
The ennui when opening the eyes, to see the truth in front of you
Hell is trivial to leave an imprint
Nipples perked and now they hurt so as my spirit dwindles

Pain

If ever it could hurt so bad
So bad if ever it could hurt
Like birth, the pain unbearable but in the end brings good things
Let me explain
If a torch shall burn, the fire should be lit
In the flame is a beautiful essence but if you touch that flame you will only feel pain
Pain; good things?
Can it be that through pain brings good things?
Tears can help you see
See yourself just a little clearer
I sit here with my mind on fire
My heart hurts
This body aches
Nevertheless, I wait for the beauty that will awaken through this pain
I say in the eye is a lie and the body can be deceiving
I say in the heart is misjudgments but the mind is not blind you'll see this in time
Until then it is one pain after the other
Another bruise to heal
More pain to feel
Until you see, what is real and real is the comfort of yourself not in the small comforts of another

J.L. Davenport

Out of Tune

I will smile the smiles I have seen
I will laugh the laughter I have heard
I will speak as I have been spoken
I will cry the tears I have dried
I will hurt, as I have been hurt and three times my pain
I will torture like so many tortures upon me and all around me
Many times my shame
I will kill and say the heavens spoke…
        Oh my brother
If you are alive then why are you dead?
You have yet to live
Repeat after me and set yourself free
My heart is broken
My spirit is sad
My body is cold and lonely
My mind is disturbed and out of tune

Ignominy

Fantasy and reality blurs
Every word echoed from thou mouth is slurs of unbecoming frenzy
You have twisted your intelligence
If you had any at all
Severe constraints is your centered frustration
You cannot comprehend thou self
Compulsive accuser
Compulsive blamer; you lack confidence
Your eyes lie; paranoia
Your eyes are truth but it is irrational to you
Stench comes instead of reason
Hideous thoughts bring forth sexual monstrosities that you cannot masturbate to please
Compelling drama
Your mind is like an HD screen and a multitude of episodes
You are weak. Say it! You are weak
Inside you have given up
Life is your enemy, fellow man is your enemy, and the world is your enemy
You! Are your enemy
Only a coward would trip with every step and deny thou self to stand tall

J.L.Davenport

Images of Unnecessary Violence
(Short story)

Let him bleed until he is dry
Black ass don't know who he's fucking with (Ha ha)
Why you run, you cannot outrun the cops
He can't answer you, just watch him bleed,
He is one less black bastard on the streets!
Turn that music down, turn it the fuck down
The copper found another thing to make him frown
Images of unnecessary violence
Ten minutes before, this young man was beating at the door
Of his girlfriend's house
A filthy house
Weeds lined the yard as small trees
Section 8 place
Would have never guessed before she moved there
"Damn bitch your shit is always dirty!" He frowns
"Well if you don't like it get the hell out!" She yells
Of course, he did not come only to go. He came to get his freak on real quick with this hoe. So he softened his voice, gave her ass a little squeeze. Telling her, "You know you're the only girl for me"
"Get the hell outta here!" She was tired of his shit
Tired of being bitches and hoes, but she knew she

was the *baddest* bitch.

So she pushed and slapped. She told him to step his ass back or she would call the police

"That's right Nigga Im'ma scream, *HE'S BEATING ME!*"

Oh, she threw herself into a wall and he said to himself that she is one crazy bitch

Then she commenced to fall flat on her face

She started to bleed and she ran out her place

How many minutes can it take a man to see that, that is not the place to be

Oops, it happened again, trap. Cause by the time he got his ass up

There were cops outside

Screaming FREEZE!

You should have seen his reaction when he opened the door. Well he wore the same reaction to the morgue

Images of unnecessary violence

J.L.Davenport

Shameful Human

It is forgetting there substance is human

It is forgetting your substance is human

It is forgetting my substance is human

Our nature as humans is to notice our differences

Sadly, that comes with a price; however, it does not have to be the price we have chosen

Deceit

Trickery

Conniving

Hate

Murder and all the suffering in between

Silk Roads of Rivers

You can't improve your life until you love your enemy... it is your enemy who suffers
Theirs is an ignorance of the core
Enough delusional grandeur to abhor
They are empowered with your hate because that is what weakens you
They will not admit the truths of the past even with the graves of thousands in their faces
Their wealth blood rung and still thriving today
Manipulator of humanity; it is killing their race
Strengthen yourself with redemption; I cannot guide you because I struggle too
Nevertheless, it is an easy price to pay
For the long awaited road where peace shall unfold

J.L.Davenport

Don't Cry Tears
Unless They Are Smiling

The diamond sparkle of the stars have crafted me in brilliance
I am like a duck gliding just above the lake
I have only gone so far if you look closely, my shadow lingers
That body that you line up to soak with tears cannot see your shudders nor hear your wailing
Take from the bouquet, you spent every cent, and pass around
      A flower here and a flower there
To the saddened and wearisome
So that my smile can paste to every face and
      Uplift the atmosphere in this place
Let me go with everlasting kisses for my stepping-stone is to deviate
From that flesh
That flesh that bound me
That mind that held me hopeless and unfocused
That heart which was broken, painfully broken and lonesome
Those eyes that could not cry and help me cope
Of the puzzle my life was bestowed
My death is a souvenir to any blessing I might have

Leakage

given

Although I go defeated…

Let me go

Forget your goodbyes and let me go

Sing, clap, and pop every limb and muscle you got with dance

Turn those tears into smiles

Remembrance into laughter

Vitality trance be it because I am alive

The dimensions of time have already molded something new

Accretion, I am just now able to see it through

Accouchement, bring forth the copulation that I might come full circle

Take me to the sky

J.L. Davenport

Spit spat

Place your frustrations in a pen

Frustrations on a pad leaking

Leaking spit

Spit the essence of a being

Every yawn every scream every conversation

It breeds

If only everyone could be, clean

Place your frustrations in a pen

Frustrations on a pad leaking

Leaking spit

Utilize imagery orchestrate vomit

Like a toilet bowl

Nasty then clean but that is only temporarily

Be thoroughgoing

Fast, slow or out of control

On paper it all goes

In the mind it will flow

Bad Taste

It is an awful thing

To sometimes be the pretty thang

To walk past a man that has not let it swang in a long while

To beg for the pussy or even ask for a taste is not his style

He's gonna take what he wants anyway

He wants you

Got a bad taste in her childhood

In his house, around his kids, his obese wife in the other room eating her sandwich and watching soaps

Funny how things can happen when you go spend the weekend with a childhood friend

You do not go back home the same girl again

Got a bad taste in her lily

Something done forced its way in

Something done had fun and run

Something done planted wasteful seed

Legs went cramped

Back is scratched

Arse is wet

Hair is mangled

Eyes burn and so does her lily

How long should she lay there? Someone might see her

J.L.Davenport

Got a bad taste in her mouth
Nausea don't come fast enough because she can't breathe
Laying there and can't close her legs
Looking at the cracked peeling ceiling
Young innocence thronged and now that is gone
Got a bad taste in her stomach
Gonna go back home and hide until it starts growing inside
Whose fault is it now?
Why didn't you say anything?
What were you doing?
How did this happen?
Now the man is dead
Whatch'u gonna to do now?
You're not gonna embarrass this family around town
I know someone who wants her
Got a bad taste into womanhood
One, two, three that is what's left of her now
The pretty young thang and her babies
Yeah, she has seen the ring
She has even traveled the world
She is a lucky girl
Live happily ever after
I do not think so
Young thang is lost, and then she is found

Leakage

It's gonna take a lot more to turn her around
She is so full of anger that is what they say
However, they do not see her on her happy days
Got a bad taste in her mind
Then something triggers her pain and abuse
Only music can cut her loose
That pen and paper sets her free
She is in her own world there and she is happy
She is her own happiness and it is a sad thing actually
She is lost in her madness and that is irrelevant to the sadness
The past has went and it's time to move on
As she said, young innocence thronged and now it is gone
She just got a bad taste

J.L.Davenport

Feel Right

When I look at you, I wish so many things
So many things I know will never be
I am aware you do not really see
That when I kiss you I dream
I dream like a schoolgirl with her first crush
Within my black skin I blush
It does not feel right that I should feel this way
About a man, I do not see every day or every month
Oh, the years will soon become few and it still feels new
When you enter into my receiving, body so close to my womb…
It is you and your deliverance
When you are pleased and you smile at me
I want more
Can you see thoroughly my needs?
You have barely touched my fervid flesh
Nor kissed and hugged me as much
Has the scent of my soft moist skin even set in?
So that in the morning you can sniff at the beauty, you began
And ended with you
The idyll light that sparkles in my eyes
I am saddened
I am not satisfied

It is tears lapping against my eyeballs
Blatant stare because I will not blink
I do not want you to see me cry
I do not want you to think
I just want you to know it does not feel right leeching
to the dream
The more I dream the stranger you become

J.L.Davenport

Pushing me away

Every day you are pushing me away
In every way, you are asking me to stay
You look into my eyes
You hold my body tight
You spend countless hours with me with ease
Every day you try to push me away
Every way you are asking me to stay and I am willing
Times have gotten hard
Burdens are stiff upon our shoulders
Massages come
Relief will go but I will take the journey
You are asking me in the hardest way to stay and I will

Eye Blink

In one blink
Time goes by so quick
It is morning then night
Does thy eye blink so slowly?
A string of incidents and I am convinced, it is I who should be sorry
To be alone is, well, lonely to say the least
Therefore, you give your heart away even if it is not easy to take
Nevertheless, the discomfort is the same
Three
Not enough to connect
Three plus thoughts plus plans stand-ups, stand-ins waiting
Torture to thy self is embarrassment
Take away loneliness and embrace bliss
It can be easily missed so you slam the door on your intuition and accept it
That small bliss that the lonely miss
Contrite
Aye says I for this is the time to grasp exaggeration and kick it in the arse
Nothing is truly ever alone
My heart was trembling though the beauty of the blood is the renewal it brings and so quickly does it

J.L.Davenport

clean

Time goes by so quick

It is morning then night does thy eye blink so slow

I can proceed as if that small bliss had not existed but

it did

Thank you

Even if my manner may not appreciate, I am ok

In one blink

Leakage

CHAPTER 3
Inequitable

J.L.Davenport

Imagine

9 months within the womb
Soft and subtle voice of comfort while you bloom
Tender pink flesh
Weak and throbbing
Push
  Push
Pushing towards the exit
Tense pasty palms, perspiring face
Affectionate; a kiss of rose puckered lips
The father looks on half embracing the woman who borne his miracle
With an ebony glow
His dark, strong hand
Your cheek he strokes
To ease the wails of newborn life
This angelic child which is white- the birth certificate reads Negro
9 months within the womb
Soft and subtle voice of comfort while you bloom
Tender olive flesh
Weak and throbbing
Push
  Push
Pushing towards the exit
Raisin hands relaxing from clenched fist

Leakage

Perspiring face

Affectionate; a kiss of thick lilac lips

The father looks on half embracing the woman who

borne his miracle

With a blushing glow

His pale, strong hand

Your cheek he strokes

To ease the wails of newborn life

This angelic child olive like- the birth certificate

reads Negro

J.L.Davenport

No Will to Forgive

This is a realization
I hate you with every breath
Even more than the word or phrase can articulate
Forehead bouncing off the cement wall three times, a body falls to the ground
Footprints leave heel to toe dancing fractures on ribs
Cement wall and your kids
There's a connection; stars
Stars that shine brighter now than ever laying here on the basement floor
Like sitting on the bridge of County 9 looking at the twinkling of the stars
In labor, the stars shined once a sea of sparkling roses when you came your hands were empty
In labor, the stars shined a big bright smile when you came you wore a frown that was of constant complaining
In labor, the stars shined an immense embrace that swathed my soul, kept me at ease and aimed to please when you came you were destined to take that away from me
Now the stars shine brighter now than ever laying here on the basement floor
Like sitting on the bridge of County 9 looking at the twinkling of the stars

I am resigned

I hate you with every breath

Even more than the word or phrase can articulate

On arrival of judgment day hells fire will have me

I am acquiescent

I have no more will to forgive

J.L.Davenport

Denazify

Law and humanity will never be on the same scale
Law does not make a human and no human has a right to say which one is human enough
When a man feels he has the power to look at another man and say you are beneath me because your skin is dark and your hair is knot
Than that is the man inferior to GOD
He is the anomaly of all humanity
He is the devil's child
Politically it means nothing to me
I speak for the respect of humanity
The act of Mankind to ignore the Laws of Nature, by reproducing offspring like a virus and not like a mammal
In regards to breeding, they do not
The child will rear alone
One child who will come from the loins of the wicked
Many from the loins of the disadvantaged
Some from the loins of the religious
Each in its own has made a home to beget criminals
So many things denied now
Denied is not better
I do not lessen any soul that has been victimized
All victims have and are eventually heard in this world without a peep

There is only one race of victims that have ceased to be heard
Scars tell a story you know
Scars heal from the inside out
However, sometimes scars only heal outside
Moreover, the healing on the inside takes time
Who has time when the world keeps going?
That is what you see in black America
That is what you see in Africa
That is what you see in the Middle East
Even the white child who will bear the faults, of the past abuses engaged towards the aught
There is no time to heal
Too many scars
Each needs time
Too many memories, too many tales, too many lies
Too much of everything
And not enough
History is written in blood
The only means to victory is destroying racism, superiority and corruptive behaviors
Can it ever be?

J.L.Davenport

Broken Limbs to Set Me Free

Scars of my brothers
Wails of my sisters
Moans of my fathers
Screams of my mothers and silence in the air
Cord of life severed
To this life you bloom
Bloom as the dandelion quick for the picking
As nutritious as it be, it only be a weed
Unappealing so it seems

Snap
   Snap
      Snap

Limbs snap on the trees with every jerk
Every jerk to the earth below is piercing
Vulgar; the leaking girth mutilated
And then the bullets to the face
A laugh not so far away
Photographers leer without a pucker just the squint
of their eyes to catch the frame with some sunlight
inside
The dead young to hang blithe, with a ravaged body
and no genitals well into the night and many days
Swinging, burning and bleeding

Leakage

Into the soil, its tangible companion
This life is no more
Dedicated to the white savages of yesteryear
May your evil have left a genetic curse and if there
were good of your seed that they may also hurt!

Depart The Past

You came as a friend
Across the oceans and seas
With pale skin like a ghost
Hair blowing in the breeze
Your smile and curious eyes
Your ships
Your attire
Seemed no threat at all
Simple adversary was not so simple
Feet blistering, I have created my own soles and you wear shoes
You drink of many wines and eat of different taste from every place I did not know were ever so close and ever so far
Profound indifference, with my rich land and dark skin
Indifference profound you saw the riches and planted trenches throughout the land and behind them, you smiled the smiles of a friend

J.L.Davenport

You wanted territory and the trickery you possessed
to rein so is new land you shall claim
Hundreds of years
The rifts between our valleys are still a magnitude
Three fifth of the constitution reflects truth that
would be me and not you and the economic milieu
has created repressed fools with dragging feet
Proverbial fashion with guns and less school, with
drugs and less food
Construed racket of repressed and then regressed
English is now the modern tongue and the tongue
that speaks so thrift and ignorant cannot even share
a definition
The past has caused this ignorance
No matter that, you find it complaint after complaint
Excuse after excuse
It is the past that still last right in the faces and in
open places
It echoes off electricity that flows from public stations
that we call entertainment
It has latched to dormant confidence and whipped it
up so much
Instead of whip cream, you have devils pie and half
the chefs cannot prepare that right
It is like a prenuptial on my life, it has been there
before the word, and the word has owned and

Leakage

destroyed me and mines
However, there is time
Time to rekindle our relationship even if the first was built on wounds
Your empty vase I have filled even if I was and am the victim
Condemn the source of racism
The ideology weakens the very soil we share as home
Fill the void and help me rediscover my spirit lost so long ago
If you stopped and opened up your mouth with no threat in your step
No indifference in your eyes
True compassion in your heart
Approach me as a man who came from a mother and a father
Approach me as a mother who gives birth and nurtures
And not as charity to an unfortunate or as you are better than me
You have only had more time
So please give me mines
If you could say these words and mean them,
"With all the hate I have shown I now offer my love I offer my time I offer my friendship in recompense
It is time to leave the past and walk into the future

J.L.Davenport

together
We have been together for so long."
I could have a chance to prosper and feel I have done so and then the land in which we share together would be a hundredths fold.

No Victim

You are not a victim father

You are not a victim sister

You are not a victim brother

You are not a victim mother

Free your mind

Free your spirit

Free yourself

The blame lies in the groins of my brothers who will leave their children behind, speak without thinking, and kill without reasoning

The blame lies in the sisters with their attire showing them loose, loud mouths and plenty of attitudes

The blame lies in the hands of the father who leaves his children to pave their own way

Now they're impoverished

Now they're proud imbeciles

Now they're truant

They are defenseless and dispensable in the eyes of others

The blame lies in the mother because unfortunately she is not superwoman

She is not superwoman

You are not a victim

Even when the world will do its damage

The lashes still being inflicted upon your back

J.L.Davenport

The lashes still being inflicted upon your back
I tell you that you are not a victim
You are not a victim father
You are not a victim sister
You are not a victim brother
You are not a victim mother
Free your mind then free your spirit and hold your head up high
When their actions become physical making you vulnerable
Or the oppressive institutions are making you miserable
Scream out to society until it pierces ears
Ha! They can only say you complain too much
So what
Scream out to society until it pierces ears
Ha! They can only say you complain too much
They will only say we complain too much
So what
Many will hear and many will see
You are not a victim!
You are not a victim!
You are not a victim father
You are not a victim sister
You are not a victim brother
You are not a victim mother

Leakage

You are the beginning of a nurtured seed

However, it will not bloom without the water

If you drug it instead of hug it

Rape it and abuse it

Disease it

Instead of nurture it and fill it with the knowledge it needs

Even before violence can take its life

Those flowering petals are going to bleed

J.L.Davenport

Mold Me

A woman crying and cradling herself over a man
Repulsive
Why doesn't she just grasp hold of his power?
He craves her warmth
Whether it be in the multitudes of flesh that will open to him
Leave that man at her mercy to dispel his frustrations and tears
Where the other boys will not hear
Fortunately, he is fragile too.
If not for his physical strength, comfort and seed
Gratification, a woman can conquer alone, mightily
Advice woman
You beautiful creature, you are God's prize
To allow a man to take your pride and keep you defeated
Absurd
Say to him, in a pleasant voice or a seductive choice
Bring his balls to his knees and let him know
The big toe has yet to blister at the thought of you mister
It was the heart chasing you and now it is broken
You're effeminate if not emasculate that you approach me with steel arms, armored torso and in detail lay upon me your perverted sense of

Leakage

entitlement

If an orgasm were the truth, well then the lie is you

Say to him, with the smile he loves

You uncouth fool

Are you happy now? Are you enjoying yourself?

Squeeze in more talking and sulking. I just want to see your handsome face, which will soon be replaced with another. Men come a dime a dozen because the rest are still boys.

Invigilate your conscience

You are already stupefied

Babble with your tongue

Your opprobrious words cannot persuade me, if I laugh, will you scream?

Say to him, only you are verbally stimulated, however you are psychologically mutilated

You have not won

Say to him, you cannot defeat me with the bass in your voice

You may very well grow hoarse

You cannot debate my defense with all your muscle and muster

I state my case; you may have delayed me with the pump of your genital

However, you will never mold me

J.L.Davenport

Leakage

! Get To Know!

J.L.Davenport

https://www.facebook.com/author.jldavenport

J.L.Davenport is a spoken word artist, author and songwriter.
She shares her perceptions on the realities of life's misgivings and dare you to open her books, view the detail of her words, and seep deep into her thoughts opening a door to truths many turn a blind eye to.

Leakage

www.ingramcontent.com/pod-product-compliance
Lightning Source LLC
Chambersburg PA
CBHW031420040426
42444CB00005B/656